SCIENCE WIDE OPEN

Women in Physics

Written by Mary Wissinger
Illustrated by Danielle Pioli

Created and edited by John J. Coveyou

Science, Naturally!
An imprint of Platypus Media, LLC
Washington, D.C.

Why do things fall down?

What an excellent question! Things fall down to the ground because the Earth pulls them toward itself. That pull is called gravity.

Émilie du Châtelet was also curious about gravity, but finding answers wasn't easy.

People talked about big ideas in cafés, but back then only men were allowed. Émilie dressed in men's clothing so she could join the conversation.

To make it tougher, the best book on things like gravity—Isaac Newton's *Principia*—was only written in Latin.

But that didn't stop a brave woman like Émilie.

7

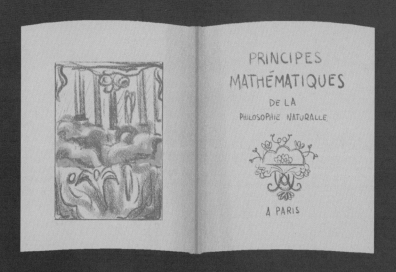

Émilie spent four years translating the entire book into French, so she could read it in her language. Her research and experiments helped her create equations and form new ideas about gravity. She got people around the world excited about physics, and her work inspired future scientists like Albert Einstein.

(France, 1706–1749)

9

That sounds important. But what's physics?

$$E = \frac{1}{2}mv^2$$

So glad you asked! Physics is the study of how and why everything in the universe moves and works. Physics helps us explain how birds can fly, or why water freezes when it's cold and turns into steam when it's hot.

On Bubbles of Air
That Escape
from Fluids

Laura Bassi
1748

Laura Bassi could tell you all about those things because she was the first woman in the world to be a professor of physics. She ran many experiments on things like bubbles, water, and fire.

Her house was full of scientific equipment, and she even gave physics lessons in her home! She loved studying force—that's the push or pull on things in the universe.

(Italy, 1711–1778)

13

Can I catch force?

No, we can't catch force or even see it.
Force is invisible.

But how can we study something we can't see?

Even though we can't see force, we can see what force does. A ball sitting in the grass stays still until you kick it. The force from your kick sends the ball sailing until the force of gravity pulls it back down to Earth.

Physicists study lots of things we can't see. They start with a question and a possible answer—that's called a hypothesis. Then they run experiments and observe the results to see if they were correct.

Radioactive Atom

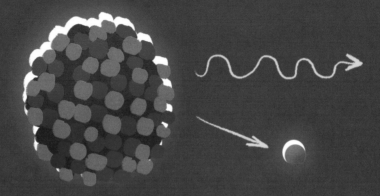

Marie Curie was famous for her experiments with radioactivity, a type of energy that can move in invisible waves.

Marie won a Nobel Prize for her work—the first one ever awarded to a woman. She kept experimenting and won another Nobel Prize for discovering two new radioactive elements: radium and polonium.

(Poland and France, 1867–1934)

19

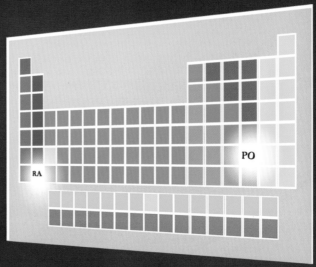

What are elements?

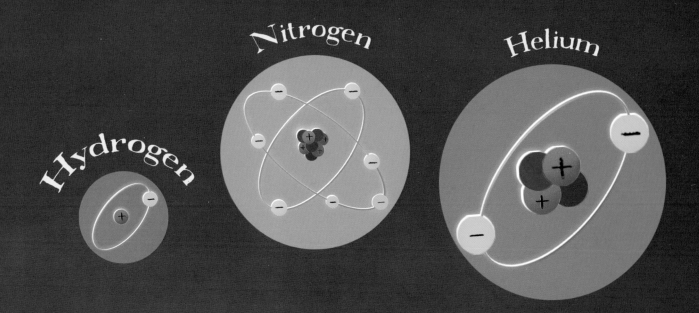

An element is the name given to each type of atom.

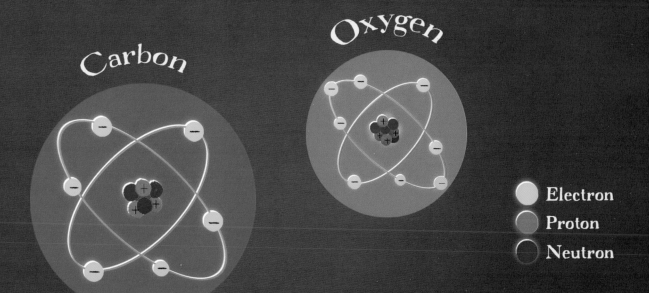

Electron
Proton
Neutron

21

You can think of atoms as tiny building blocks that make up everything in the universe.

Marie and her daughter Irene Joliot-Curie dedicated their lives to studying elements and radioactivity.

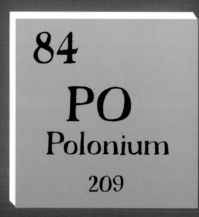

84

PO

Polonium

209

Sometimes Irene was so focused that she forgot
to say hello to other lab workers. She spent years
conducting experiments, especially with the
element polonium that her mom discovered.

Irene's hard work paid off though, and she won a
Nobel Prize for research, too! Marie and Irene were
the first parent and child to both win Nobel Prizes
for their discoveries.

I want to discover something!

You can!

We're always learning new things about how the universe works, but it takes patience and lots of hard work to make discoveries.

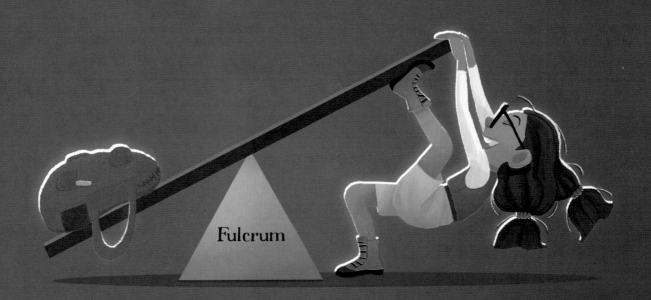

Fulcrum

Just look at Chien-Shiung Wu. Her name meant "Courageous Hero," but she was more than that. She fearlessly asked big questions and ran complex experiments to find the answers.

Chien-Shiung loved doing careful work and making observations. She helped make a discovery that surprised the world.

(China and United States, 1912–1997)

Cool! How'd she do that?

Well, people thought they knew exactly what happened when atoms fall apart, but they were wrong. Chien-Shiung's experiment showed something completely different! Her results were so amazing that it changed the way people looked at physics. It was like she dropped something up instead of down!

That's really incredible!

But... we know that things fall to the ground, because of gravity.

You're right.

But a scientist like you can double check by making a hypothesis, conducting an experiment, and observing the results. That way, you can make your own discoveries, too!

Can you find...?

Émilie du Châtelet (EM-i-lee du SHAH-tuh-leh)

Laura Bassi (LAH-rah BAH-see)

Marie Curie (MAH-ree CURE-ee)

Irene Joliot-Curie (EE-ren ZHOH-lee-oh CURE-ee)

Chien-Shiung Wu (chyen shyung woo)

Glossary

ATOMS: The building blocks that put together our universe. Different kinds of atoms are made by combining different numbers of protons, neutrons, and electrons.

EINSTEIN, ALBERT: One of the most famous scientists in history, known for his theories of relativity (which changed our understanding of gravity) and mass-energy equivalence ($E=mc^2$). He was born in 1879 in Germany, received his education in Italy, and moved to the U.S. in 1933.

ELECTRONS: Very teeny particles with a negative electric charge. Electrons travel around the nucleus of every atom.

ELEMENT: A basic substance made of one type of atom that usually cannot be separated into simpler substances.

ENERGY: The cause of any movement or change. The greatest source of energy on Earth is the Sun. Other forms of energy include thermal, mechanical, electrical, chemical, gravitational, sound, and nuclear.

EXPERIMENT: A test to collect information about the world to see if a hypothesis is correct.

FORCE: The push or pull on something when it interacts with something else. A force can cause an object to move faster, slow down, stay in place, or change shape.

FULCRUM: The pivotal point that supports the movement of a lever, such as the center point of a see-saw.

GRAVITY: A force that attracts ALL objects toward each other. This force gets bigger as the objects get bigger, which is why our bodies feel the force of gravity from the Earth, but not from a spoon or apple.

HYPOTHESIS: An educated guess that a person makes to explain something they think is true or will happen.

MASS: A measure of how much matter is in an object. Mass is usually measured in kilograms (1 kg = a little over 2 pounds). Mass is different from weight because the mass of an object never changes, but its weight will change based on its location in the universe.

MATTER: Anything that takes up space and has mass.

NEUTRONS: Very teeny particles with no electric charge, found in the nucleus of most atoms.

NEWTON, ISAAC: An English physicist and mathematician credited with the development of calculus and modern physics, including the laws of motion and the theory of gravity. He was born in 1642 and published his most important work, the *Principia*, in 1687.

NOBEL PRIZE: A set of very prestigious annual international awards recognizing academic, cultural, and scientific advances. The awards are named for Swedish scientist Alfred Nobel, and were first awarded in 1895.

OBSERVATION: Using our senses to collect information about the world around us.

PHYSICS: The study of matter and energy, and how they interact. Physicists observe everything from tiny particles to the whole universe, and use mathematics to develop theories for why certain things happen.

RADIOACTIVITY: The particles and energy an atom gives off when its nucleus is broken apart. It is measured in a unit called the "curie," abbreviated as "Ci," after Marie Curie and her physicist husband, Pierre Curie.

RESEARCH: To investigate and study something in order to learn new things about it.

X-RAY: Invisible waves of energy that can pass through solid objects. X-ray images can show the inside of an object, like a suitcase or a person's body.

Science Wide Open: Women in Physics
Copyright © 2021, 2019, 2016 Genius Games, LLC
Originally published by Genius Games, LLC in 2016

Written by Mary Wissinger
Illustrated by Danielle Pioli
Created and edited by John J. Coveyou

Published by Science, Naturally!
English hardback first edition • 2016 • ISBN: 978-1-945779-11-4
       Second edition • November 2019
English paperback first edition • April 2021 • ISBN: 978-1-938492-34-1
English eBook first edition • 2016 • ISBN: 978-1-945779-14-5
       Second edition • November 2019
Spanish paperback first edition • April 2021 • ISBN: 978-1-938492-35-8
Spanish eBook first edition • April 2021 • ISBN: 978-1-938492-36-5

Enjoy all the titles in the series:
       Women in Biology • Las mujeres en la biología
       Women in Chemistry • Las mujeres en la química
       Women in Physics • Las mujeres en la física
              More titles coming soon!

Teacher's Guide available at the Educational Resources page of ScienceNaturally.com.

Published in the United States by:
       Science, Naturally!
              An imprint of Platypus Media, LLC
       725 8th Street, SE, Washington, D.C. 20003
       202-465-4798 • Fax: 202-558-2132
       Info@ScienceNaturally.com • ScienceNaturally.com

Distributed to the trade by:
       National Book Network (North America)
              301-459-3366 • Toll-free: 800-462-6420
              CustomerCare@NBNbooks.com • NBNbooks.com
       NBN international (worldwide)
              NBNi.Cservs@IngramContent.com • Distribution.NBNi.co.uk

Library of Congress Control Number: 2020921218

10 9 8 7 6 5 4 3 2 1

Printed in Canada

"For trailblazing women everywhere."
—Mary Wissinger

"For all the curious minds, those who are
always open and ready to expand."
—Danielle Pioli

Download the free Teacher's Guide for further reading,
hands-on activities, and more information.

Access it at ScienceNaturally.com/Educational-Resources.

Discover the Science Wide Open series!

Hardback: $14.99 • Paperback: $12.95 • eBook: $11.99

8.25 x 8.25″ • 40 pages • Ages 7–10

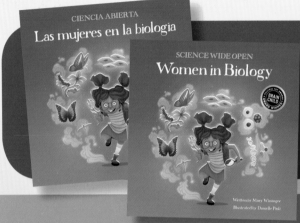

Book 1
Women in Biology
Hardback ISBN: 978-1-945779-09-1
Paperback ISBN: 978-1-938492-30-3
Spanish Paperback ISBN: 978-1-938492-07-5

Book 2
Women in Chemistry
Hardback ISBN: 978-1-945779-10-7
Paperback ISBN: 978-1-938492-31-0
Spanish Paperback ISBN: 978-1-938492-32-7

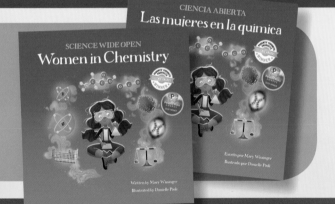

Book 3
Women in Physics
Hardback ISBN: 978-1-945779-11-4
Paperback ISBN: 978-1-938492-34-1
Spanish Paperback ISBN: 978-1-938492-35-8

ScienceNaturally.com
Info@ScienceNaturally.com

Science, Naturally! | Sparking curiosity through reading